Too Old for the Chorus

But Not Too Old to Be a Star

A Musical Revue

Book, Music and Lyrics by
Marie Cain, Mark Winkler, & Shelly Markham

Conceived by Mark Winkler

Additional Material suggested by
Jill K. Mesaros and Paula Kalustian

A SAMUEL FRENCH ACTING EDITION

NEW YORK HOLLYWOOD LONDON TORONTO

SAMUELFRENCH.COM

Copyright © 2010 by Marie Cain, Mark Winkler, Shelly Markham

ALL RIGHTS RESERVED

Cover image © 2010 Martin Kreloff

CAUTION: Professionals and amateurs are hereby warned that *TOO OLD FOR THE CHORUS, BUT NOT TOO OLD TO BE A STAR* is subject to a Licensing Fee. It is fully protected under the copyright laws of the United States of America, the British Commonwealth, including Canada, and all other countries of the Copyright Union. All rights, including professional, amateur, motion picture, recitation, lecturing, public reading, radio broadcasting, television and the rights of translation into foreign languages are strictly reserved. In its present form the play is dedicated to the reading public only.

The amateur and professional live stage performance rights to *TOO OLD FOR THE CHORUS, BUT NOT TOO OLD TO BE A STAR* are controlled exclusively by Samuel French, Inc., and licensing arrangements and performance licenses must be secured well in advance of presentation. PLEASE NOTE that amateur Licensing Fees are set upon application in accordance with your producing circumstances. When applying for a licensing quotation and a performance license please give us the number of performances intended, dates of production, your seating capacity and admission fee. Licensing Fees are payable one week before the opening performance of the play to Samuel French, Inc., at 45 W. 25th Street, New York, NY 10010.

Licensing Fee of the required amount must be paid whether the play is presented for charity or gain and whether or not admission is charged.

Stock/professional licensing fees quoted upon application to Samuel French, Inc.

For all other rights than those stipulated above, apply to: Robert A. Freedman Dramatic Agency, 1501 Broadway, Suite 2310, New York, NY 10036; attn: Selma Luttinger.

Particular emphasis is laid on the question of amateur or professional readings, permission and terms for which must be secured in writing from Samuel French, Inc.

Copying from this book in whole or in part is strictly forbidden by law, and the right of performance is not transferable.

Whenever the play is produced the following notice must appear on all programs, printing and advertising for the play: "Produced by special arrangement with Samuel French, Inc."

Due authorship credit must be given on all programs, printing and advertising for the play.

ISBN 978-0-573-69904-7   Printed in U.S.A.   #29714

No one shall commit or authorize any act or omission by which the copyright of, or the right to copyright, this play may be impaired.

No one shall make any changes in this play for the purpose of production.

Publication of this play does not imply availability for performance. Both amateurs and professionals considering a production are strongly advised in their own interests to apply to Samuel French, Inc., for written permission before starting rehearsals, advertising, or booking a theatre.

No part of this book may be reproduced, stored in a retrieval system, or transmitted in any form, by any means, now known or yet to be invented, including mechanical, electronic, photocopying, recording, videotaping, or otherwise, without the prior written permission of the publisher.

RENTAL MATERIALS

An orchestration consisting of **Piano/Vocal Score, Keyboard 2, Drums, Bass,** and **Woodwind** will be loaned two months prior to the production ONLY on the receipt of the Licensing Fee quoted for all performances, the rental fee and a refundable deposit.

Please contact Samuel French for perusal of the music materials as well as a performance license application.

IMPORTANT BILLING AND CREDIT REQUIREMENTS

All producers of *TOO OLD FOR THE CHORUS, BUT NOT TOO OLD TO BE A STAR must* give credit to the Author of the Play in all programs distributed in connection with performances of the Play, and in all instances in which the title of the Play appears for the purposes of advertising, publicizing or otherwise exploiting the Play and/or a production. The name of the Author *must* appear on a separate line on which no other name appears, immediately following the title and *must* appear in size of type not less than fifty percent of the size of the title type.

TOO OLD FOR THE CHORUS, BUT NOT TOO OLD TO BE A STAR had its world premiere in Los Angeles in March 1999 at the Celebration Theatre (Bob Schrock, Artistic Director). The performance was directed by Bob Schrock and choreographed by Chrissy Bucchino, with musical direction by Bill Schneider, lighting design by Frank McKown, and costume deisgn by Mia Gyzander. The production stage manager was Seanne Farmer, and the press representative was Kenny Werther. The cast was as follows:

BOBBY . . . . Sammy Williams
FAITH . . . . Ginny McMath
ALVIN . . . . Alvin Ing
WAYNE . . . . Wayne Moore
SHIRLEY . . . . Jo Hinds

TOO OLD FOR THE CHORUS, BUT NOT TOO OLD TO BE A STAR was produced by Jill K. Mesaros, Producing Director and CEO of Miracle Theatre Productions, at the Theatre of the Old Town, San Diego, California in 2006. The performance was directed by Paula Kalustian and choreographed by Steve Anthony, with musical direction by Lisa Lemay, arrangements by Geoff Stradling, sets by David Fredrick Weiner, costumes by Jill K. Mesaros, and sound by Chris Luessman. The cast was as follows:

BOBBY . . . . Steve Anthony
FAITH . . . . Susan Jordan De Leon
JAMES . . . . Brian Byers
GLENN . . . . David Holmes
SHIRLEY . . . . Teri Ralston
UNDERSTUDIES . . . . Bebe Brody, Rolly Fanton, Joe Savant

TOO OLD FOR THE CHORUS, BUT NOT TOO OLD TO BE A STAR was also produced by Cathy Rigby and Tom McCoy of Rigby McCoy Entertainment at La Mirada Theatre for the Performing Arts in September 2007. The performance was directed by Joel Bishoff, with sets by John Iacovelli, choreography by Dana Solimando, musical direction by Lisa Lemay, lighting by Neil Peter Jampolis, props by Terry Hanrahan, costumes by Julie Keen, sound by David Edwards, and casting by Julia Flores. The production assistant stage manager was Lea Chazin. The cast was as follows:

BOBBY . . . . Robert Loftin
FAITH . . . . Diane Vincent
JAMES . . . . Robert Yacko
GLENN . . . . David Holmes
SHIRLEY . . . . Eileen Barnett

CHARACTERS

SHIRLEY – 58-65. A beautiful life force who's "been there and done that" and still has lots of life to live - because to her, "Age Is Just A Number." A cross between Shirley MacLaine and Elaine Stritch.

BOBBY – 50. A Broadway gypsy whose body is starting to wear out, so he's pondering his options. Boyishly handsome, well-dressed and gay – he still can dance and knock 'em dead.

GLENN – 58-65. A former surfing star – now a little out of shape who welcomes the anonymity that age and a belly has given him. An optimist all the way, the martini glass is always half full to him.

FAITH – 45. A spunky former fire-baton-twirling Miss Ohio. Her husband recently left her for a younger woman and her two kids are in college. She's looking for a new beginning. Age has handed her the unexpected challenge of early menopause.

JAMES – 50-55. A former business whiz-kid who is losing out to the techno-savvy generation. Three strikes in the marriage department and his mental acuity is starting to go. Think James Naughton or Tom Wopat.

BARRY – Young. A barista at the coffee shop. He has no lines, but responds to lines and does certain stage business.

SETTING

A "retro" coffee shop with a counter up right and three stools, two tables with two chairs in front of the counter. Downstage right is a comfy chair with side table and against the stage wall is an upright piano. On stage left is a large window with a window seat. Downstage of the window seat is a couch and coffee table. Upstage center is an area for the band. The walls are decorated with items of nostalgia from the 50s and 60s – record albums, T-shirts, posters, cereal boxes, sports memorabilia etc. Magazines and newspapers are scattered on various coffee tables. There is a counter where the Barista takes orders and works. Most of the action takes place here, but there are some locations outside the coffee shop.

AUTHOR'S NOTE

For more information about the play, please visit:
www.TooOldForTheChorus.com.

MUSICAL NUMBERS

Every Seven Seconds	COMPANY
Memory Moment	SHIRLEY, JAMES
Menopause Rag	FAITH
Invisible	BOBBY, JAMES, GLENN
Latebloomers Samba	FAITH, FAITH'S MOM, BOBBY, BOBBY'S DAD
Mad As Hell	JAMES, BOBBY, GLENN
Crush	FAITH, MEN
The Road Not Taken	SHIRLEY
Yogarobics	FAITH, MEN
Dog Passages	GLENN
Age Is Just A Number	SHIRLEY, COMPANY
Lunch Hour Lift	SHIRLEY, FAITH
Child Is Father To The Man	JAMES, JAMES' DAD
When Fifty Wore A Tux	BOBBY
Too Old for the Chorus	COMPANY
MEN-O-Pause	GLENN, JAMES, FAITH
Quiet Fire	BOBBY, SHIRLEY
Potential	COMPANY
Curtain Calls: Age is Just a Number	COMPANY

1. EVERY SEVEN SECONDS

(Before the audience is seated, **ROBERT** *is sitting at one of the tables working on his laptop,* **SHIRLEY** *is reading a magazine at one of the comfy chairs, and* **BOBBY** *is seated at the window seat. The audience is then seated. After a few minutes,* **GLENN** *enters and sits at the counter and orders his drink from* **BARRY** *the barista. Then* **FAITH** *enters, gets her coffee order from* **BARRY** *and sits on the sofa.)*

JAMES.
EVERY SEVEN SECONDS
ANOTHER BABY BOOMER'S TURNING FIFTY

BOBBY.
THEN SEVEN SECONDS LATER
THAT BOOMER GETS A LETTER FROM
AARP, SAYING…

BOBBY, JAMES & FAITH.
"DEAR POTENTIAL MEMBER
THIS IS TO INFORM YOU
THAT YOU ARE OFFICIALLY OLD"

GLENN & SHIRLEY.
LOOK WHO'S ON THE COVER
OF THEIR MONTHLY MAGAZINE

ALL.
JOHN TRAVOLTA!

BOBBY.
THERE MUST BE SOME MISTAKE
BECAUSE WHEN I WAS TWENTY-THREE

BOBBY & JAMES.
HE WAS THE SAME AGE AS ME

GLENN & JAMES.   **SHIRLEY & FAITH.**
   CATALOGUES, CATALOGUES   BROCHURES!
   WE GET LOTS OF CATALOGUES   BROCHURES!

SHIRLEY.
> NO THANKS FOR THE FLANNEL NIGHTGOWN
> I'LL PASS ON THE SENSIBLE SHOES

GLENN.
> I DON'T WANT A SCALE THAT TALKS TO ME
> AND ANNOUNCES WHAT I NEED TO LOSE

FAITH. *(reading from her magazine)*
> ESTROGEN REPLACEMENT – PATCHES OR PILLS?
> I CAN'T READ THE FINE PRINT – DOES THIS SAY IT KILLS?

SHIRLEY.
> SO GO WITH ACUPUNCTURE

FAITH. Puncture?! No!
> AROMATHERAPY
> SOUNDS VERY GOOD TO ME

SHIRLEY & FAITH.
> DEAR POTENTIAL USERS
> THIS IS TO REMIND YOU
> THAT YOU ARE OFFICIALLY OLD

BOBBY & GLENN.
> EVERY SEVEN SECONDS
> ANOTHER BABY BOOMER'S TURNING FIFTY

SHIRLEY & JAMES.
> EVERY SEVEN SECONDS
> EVERY SEVEN SECONDS

FAITH, BOBBY & GLENN.
> EVERY SEVEN SECONDS
> ANOTHER BABY BOOMER'S TURNING FIFTY

SHIRLEY & JAMES.
> EVERY SEVEN SECONDS

BOBBY.
> NO SALE ON THE BARCALOUNGER

JAMES.
>DON'T SEND THE ADJUSTABLE BED

GLENN.
>HOLD OFF ON THE THREE-WHEELED SCOOTER

BOBBY, JAMES & GLENN.
>OR A PLACE WE CAN REST WHEN WE'RE DEAD

COMPANY.
>IT'S AMAZING HOW THEY FIND US
>HOW EAGER THEY ARE TO REMIND US
>THAT OUR VERY BEST DAYS ARE BEHIND US
>TIME TO SLOW DOWN AND RELAX

FAITH & SHIRLEY.
>SLOW DOWN, RELAX

ALL.
>SPEND YOUR MONEY WHILE YOU FACE THE FACTS THAT…
>EVERY SEVEN SECONDS
>ANOTHER BABY BOOMER'S TURNING FIFTY
>AND THE ONLY QUESTION IS
>IN THIS CRAZY WORLD WE LIVE IN
>DO WE FIGHT IT OR JUST GIVE IN?
>NOW THAT WE ARE OFFICIALLY OLD
>'CAUSE IT'S EVERY SEVEN SECONDS

2. MEMORY MOMENT

(**BOBBY**, **FAITH** and **GLENN** *are at the counter;* **JAMES** *and* **SHIRLEY** *are at the couch.*)

BOBBY. *(seated at counter with* **GLENN** *and* **FAITH***)* Shit, I'm late for an audition.

GLENN. I'll drink your latte for you.

BOBBY. No you won't, I'm taking it with me.

FAITH. Barry – caffeinate me please. Barry. Java Boy? Where is he?

(**FAITH** *gets up and goes looking for him – getting more agitated, then screams.*)

BARRY!!!!

JAMES. I think she's had enough coffee...

(reading from a brochure)

Well, here's a bizarre concept – the Disney Cruise Line Senior Special package.

SHIRLEY. Oh, yes! My husband booked us on that last summer – it was spectacular.

JAMES. I'll bet. What could be more exciting than a game of shuffleboard with Pluto and Goofy?

SHIRLEY. Don't be silly. I'll have you know it was all very grownup and extremely romantic.

JAMES. Where'd you go? Never Never Land?

SHIRLEY. As a matter of fact, we did go to a few places we'd never visited before. I discovered some erogenous zones I didn't even know I had. Now if I could just remember where I put them...

I USED TO BE SO GOOD AT COCKTAIL CHAT
KNOWING PEOPLE'S FIRST NAMES AT FIRST SIGHT
WHETHER TO CALL THEM PATRICK OR PAT
KEEPING THE REPARTEÉ LIGHT

WHEN THERE WAS A LULL, I'D TELL AN ANECDOTE
BUT THE PUNCHLINE WAS NOTHING YOU COULD QUOTE
I KNEW ENDLESS STORIES AND TOLD THEM WITH VERVE
THE SMALLEST DETAIL NEVER THREW ME A CURVE

SHIRLEY. *(cont.)*
NOW MY KEEN MIND SKIPS A BEAT
I CAN'T THINK OF WORDS, A PLACE OR STREET
EVEN THE SMALL STUFF IS ROUGH ON MY BRAIN
MY SYNAPSES ARE PLAYING A GAME
IT'S A PHENOMENON THAT HAS NO NAME
UNTIL NOW, 'CAUSE I'VE NAMED IT MYSELF

Oh god, what was the name of it? It was so cute – without being precious. Oh, just give me a second!

PARDON ME, BUT I'M HAVING A MEMORY MOMENT
I CAN'T RECALL WHAT I CALLED YOU A MINUTE AGO
GUESS MY AGE IS BEGINNING TO SHOW
ON THE INSIDE
MY TONGUE ISN'T TIED
OR HAVING A FIT
I KNOW EVERY BIT
THEN SUDDENLY ZIP
IT'S OFF OF THE TIP OF MY TONGUE
LIKE A VANISHING BLIP
LIKE A WALL THAT I'VE SUDDENLY HIT
WHAT THE HELL WAS THE NAME OF THAT –

Shit!

OH, WELL – PARDON ME
BUT I'M HAVING A MEMORY MOMENT

JAMES. Believe me, I know exactly how you feel. I was once on a first-name basis with Alex Trebek.

I TRULY WAS THE MASTER OF ALL TRIVIA
KNOWING FACTS THAT NO ONE EVER KNEW
ANNUAL INCOME IN BOLIVIA
WAS MATA HARI A JEW?

THE CITIES IN MOZAMBIQUE THAT END IN VOWELS
THE NAMES IN GREEK FOR MAMMALS WITHOUT BOWELS
ON JEOPARDY, I WAS SO FEARED AS THE CHAMP
THE FINGERS OF FELLOW CONTESTANTS WOULD CRAMP

Then one day my brain froze on 'Potpourri' for a thousand and I never recovered.

JAMES. *(cont.)*
I'VE BEEN TOLD THAT THERE'S A PILL
A MAGICAL BREW TO CURE MY ILL
A NATURAL HERB TO RESTORE MY BRAIN
SO I WON'T THINK I'VE GONE INSANE
IT'S AN ELIXIR WITH A FUNNY NAME
AND I CAN'T RECOLLECT WHAT IT'S CALLED

("Jeopardy"-type music underscores dialogue.)

It's the name of a lizard – I'm pretty sure it starts with a "G."

SHIRLEY. A gila monster?

JAMES. No. A hard "G."

SHIRLEY. An iguana!

JAMES. Nooooo.

SHIRLEY. A gecko.

JAMES. Yes! But not just a gecko; it's a gecko explorer. Gecko Cortez? No…

SHIRLEY. Gecko De Leon?

JAMES. Uh uh.

SHIRLEY. Gecko Magellan?

JAMES. Nope. Gecko Balboa – that's it!

SHIRLEY. You mean Gingko Biloba?

JAMES. That's what I said. Didn't I?

SHIRLEY.
PARDON ME, BUT YOU'RE HAVING A MEMORY MOMENT
YOU CAN'T THINK OF WHAT YOU THOUGHT OF A MINUTE AGO

JAMES.
YES, MY PANIC IS STARTING TO GROW
ON THE INSIDE
MY NOODLE AIN'T FRIED
I SIMPLY FORGOT
TO FINISH A THOUGHT
AND NOW I AM CAUGHT
OUT HERE WITH MY BUTT ON THE LINE

JAMES. *(cont.)*
AND I'M SUDDENLY STRUCK
LIKE I'M HIT BY AN ALZHEIMER'S TRUCK
WHAT THE HELL WAS THE NAME OF THAT –

(slapping his forehead)

Schmuck!

OH WELL, PARDON ME
OH HELL, PARDON ME
BUT I'M HAVING A MEMORY…MOMENT

SHIRLEY. *(singing)*

I…

(pauses, considering)

…USED TO BE SO GOOD AT COCKTAIL CHAT

JAMES. *(spoken)* Knowing people's first names at first sight?

SHIRLEY. Yes! How did you know?

(pause)

SHIRLEY & JAMES. *(sung)*
OH. WELL PARDON ME, BUT WE'RE HAVING A MEMORY MOMENT.

3. MENOPAUSE RAG

(**FAITH** *crosses to center and the lights fade on the rest of the coffee shop.*)

FAITH. Hey!
IS IT HOT IN HERE, OR IS IT ONLY ME?
IS IT THE NIACIN, IS IT THE MSG?
OR THE RESULT OF HORMONE THERAPY?
OR IS IT THE MENOPAUSE RAG?

DON'T TOUCH ME NOW – I'M NOT IN THE MOOD
AND I AM WARNING YOU THAT I CAN GET REAL RUDE
I WANT SOME HÄAGEN-DAZS; I WANT ITALIAN FOOD
DOIN' THE MENOPAUSE RAG

GET ME SOME PROZAC; GET ME SOME BRANDY
GET ME A POUND OF CHOCOLATE CANDY
A HEATING PAD WOULD COME IN HANDY
AN ICE PACK WOULD BE FINE AND DANDY

DON'T TRY FORCE OR FLATTERY
DON'T TRY TO FIGURE OUT WHAT'S THE MATTER WITH ME
JUST BUY ME A SUPPLY OF BATTERIES
'CAUSE I'M DOIN' THE MENOPAUSE
CHEWIN' UP MEN BECAUSE
I'M DOING THE MENOPAUSE RAG

Somebody open a freakin' window!

4. INVISIBLE/INVINCIBLE

(**JAMES** *is at Stage Right table,* **BOBBY** *is Stage Left table and* **GLENN** *is at the counter.* **FAITH** *is at the window seat.*)

JAMES. Y'know…I envy women. They have that built-in alarm clock that tells them they're getting older. How are we supposed to know when it starts happening to us?

BOBBY. When no matter what you wear, it takes twice as long to look half as good.

JAMES. How about when you see your reflection in a store window and you think, "Who is that old fart?" And you realize…

JAMES & BOBBY. It's you!

BOBBY.
LATELY THE AUDITIONS ARE THE SAME
AND WHEN THEY READ THE LIST OF CALLBACKS
WELL, I NEVER HEAR MY NAME
NO ONE WANTS A GUY WITH ALL THIS WEAR AND TEAR
MY LEOTARDS ARE OLDER
THAN HALF THOSE KIDS OUT THERE

I'M TOO OLD FOR THE CHORUS
A BRONTOSAURUS ON THE STAGE
IT'S JUST THE BOYS THAT ALL GET OLDER NOW
THE LEADING LADIES NEVER AGE

JUST WHEN I'VE LEARNED EV'RY STEP OF THE DANCE
NO ONE IS WILLING TO GIVE ME A CHANCE

I AM INVISIBLE
AND NOW THEY LOOK RIGHT PAST ME
I'M INVISIBLE
TO THE ONES WHO USED TO CAST ME
EVERY GUY WHO ONCE WENT "WOW!"
WON'T EVEN SEE ME NOW
I AM INVISIBLE

(*Music changes to a driving rock beat.*)

JAMES.
>WHEN I WAS A YOUNG TURK
>JUST STARTIN' IN BUSINESS
>SO FULL OF AMBITION
>AND JUNIOR GEE-WHIZNESS
>AS FEARLESS AS I COULD BE
>WITH A CHARMINGLY RUTHLESS DRIVE
>AND EVERYONE TOUTING ME
>AS A GENIUS AT TWENTY-FIVE
>
>I MADE UP MY OWN RULES
>AND RACED UP THE LADDER
>I TRAMPLED SOME OLD FOOLS
>BUT WHAT DID IT MATTER?
>THE POWER THAT COMES WITH FAME
>WHAT A CRUEL APHRODISIAC
>IT BLINDED ME TO THE GAME
>I FORGOT HOW TO WATCH MY BACK
>
>THEY SAID THERE'D BE PAYBACK ONE OF THESE DAYS
>THE NEW KID ON BOARD IS GETTIN' THE RAISE
>
>I AM INVISIBLE
>THEY SEEM TO LOOK RIGHT THROUGH ME
>I'M INVISIBLE
>AND WHILE THEY'RE TALKIN' TO ME
>IT'S TRUE, THEY CALL ME 'SIR'
>BUT NOW IT'S LIKE A SLUR
>I AM INVISIBLE
>
>WHEN DID THE MOMENT HAPPEN?

BOBBY.
>HOW DID THE PICTURE CHANGE?

JAMES & BOBBY.
>WHO IS THAT MAN IN THE MIRROR?
>WHY DOES HE LOOK SO STRANGE?
>WHEN DID THE BRIGHT YOUNG BOY
>ON EVERYONE'S LIST
>CEASE TO EXIST?
>
>*(Music changes to a jazzy bossa nova.)*

GLENN. Stop! All this negativity is downright depressing. Things change, go with it. If you can't play the old game, take up a new one – like I did. So I can't surf anymore – now I fish or play golf; sports that involve cocktails.

I WAS THE KAHUNA
THE KING OF THE OCEAN
THE OBJECT OF ENVY
AND BOUNDLESS DEVOTION
AND EVERYBODY FOUGHT TO SEE
EVERY INCH OF MY SUNTANNED SKIN
ALL MY HAIR WAS WHERE IT OUGHT TO BE
I HAD A CLEFT IN MY SINGLE FLAWLESS CHIN

I'D SHOW OFF MY MUSCLES
TO DRIVE THE GIRLS CRAZY
I BATTED A THOUSAND
BUT THEN I GOT LAZY

MY BELLY GOT BIGGER THAN ALL MY ACCLAIM
AND NOW THEY DON'T EVEN REMEMBER MY NAME

I AM INVISIBLE, INVISIBLE
THERE'S NO MORE SCORING
NO WORSHIP AND ADORING
BUT LIFE IS GOOD BECAUSE
I AM INVISIBLE, INVISIBLE
SINCE I'VE BEEN SHUT OUT
NOW I CAN LET MY GUT OUT
AND NO ONE SEES MY FLAWS
I AM INVISIBLE

And y'know, it's a funny thing…the bigger I get, the more invisible I become. Ironic, isn't it? I mean, – who did we all want to be when we were kids??

BOBBY. Fred Astaire.

JAMES. Lee Iacocca.

GLENN. No – The Invisible Man! Okay, so it was mostly because we wanted to spy on girls. Right?

JAMES. Oh yeah – there was that.

BOBBY. Like I said, I wanted to be Fred Astaire.

GLENN. Oh. Okay. Anyway, my point is this: I'm tired of being invisible – we need to be invincible!

JAMES. How do you figure?

GLENN. Sheer numbers. In surfer terms, the first wave of Boomers is just startin' to hit the shore. And when the second wave comes in behind it…Dudes! We're gonna be impossible to ignore.

THERE ARE INCREDIBLE THINGS TO BE DONE

BOBBY.
IF WE ALL WISE UP AND RISE UP AS ONE

GLENN & BOBBY.
WE'LL BE INVINCIBLE

GLENN.
LIKE THREE PYRAMIDS STILL STANDING

GLENN & BOBBY.
INVINCIBLE

BOBBY.
SO SOLID AND COMMANDING
'CAUSE WE'VE LEARNED A THING OR TWO

JAMES.
STAND BACK AND LET US THROUGH

ALL.
WE'LL BE INVINCIBLE

JAMES.
LIKE SUPERMAN GONE SENIOR

ALL.
INVINCIBLE

BOBBY.
AND CONQUERING EACH LEAN YEAR

GLENN.
THOUGH WE CAN'T FLY THROUGH THE AIR

ALL.
WE'RE HEROES WITH GREY HAIR
WE ARE INVINCIBLE
WE WON'T JUST DISAPPEAR
WE'RE INVINCIBLE
AND WE'RE STILL HERE!

5. LATEBLOOMER'S SAMBA

(**FAITH** *is at window seat,* **BOBBY** *is at counter,* **JAMES** *is on sofa.*)

(*Music underscoring. A phone rings.* **FAITH** *answers it.*)

FAITH. Hello?

(**FAITH'S MOM [SHIRLEY]** *enters with a sunchair from Stage Right and sits right center.*)

FAITH'S MOM (SHIRLEY). Hello, Faith. It's Mom. Just wondering if you've given any more thought to going back to school.

FAITH. Well, not really…

FAITH'S MOM. You need to think about it, honey. You know, you can't earn a living being a homemaker…

FAITH. Unless you're Martha Stewart. I know, Mom.

FAITH'S MOM. And with both kids in college and that inadequate alimony…I still can't believe Phil actually married that 18 year-old dental assistant of his.

FAITH. She's 23.

FAITH'S MOM. To think, when you were 23, you were Second Runner Up to Miss Michigan.

FAITH. Well, it's too late to capitalize on that. Not much call for fire-baton twirling. I just don't know what I want to be.

FAITH'S MOM. Why don't you become a psychologist? You're a very good listener.

FAITH. Mom, that takes four years! I'd be 54 years old when I got my degree!

FAITH'S MOM. And how old will you be in four years if you don't get a degree?

(*A phone rings.* **BOBBY** *answers it.*)

BOBBY. Hello?

(**BOBBY'S DAD** *enters from Stage Left on a treadmill.*)

BOBBY'S DAD (GLENN). Hello, Bobby! It's your father. I just got back from Boca. You'll never guess who I ran into at the hotel buffet – Bernice! You know, her son is a big shot orthopedic surgeon down there.

BOBBY. Yes, Dad. I do know that.

BOBBY'S DAD. Well, did you know that he nets a million dollars a year? Without even trying! You know, Bobby…it's not too late for you to change careers. You can't dance forever.

BOBBY. Thanks for reminding me, Dad.

BOBBY'S DAD. You're welcome. You know I'm just concerned about your future.

BOBBY. I understand that – but I'm certainly not going to be an orthopedic surgeon. Although it would be nice to be able to do my own hip and knee replacements.

BOBBY'S DAD. Listen, I know you have the ability to be anything you want to be. Even at this late age.

(Music begins with a drum break, hot Latin rhythms.)

BOBBY.
> MY DAD ALWAYS SAYS TO ME
> I AM CERTAIN YOU WILL BE A LATE BLOOMER

FAITH.
> DARLING, IT'S YOUR DESTINY
> PEOPLE IN OUR FAMILY ARE LATE BLOOMERS.

BOBBY.
> EV'RY TIME I GET A PHONE CALL OR A LETTER
> HE REMINDS ME THAT I COULD BE DOING BETTER

FAITH.
> BUT MY CLOCK IS TICKIN'
> AND I'M ALMOST PANIC STRICKEN
> I SAY MAMA, I'LL BE BLOOMING IN MY GRAVE.

BOBBY & FAITH.
> BUT THAT BRAVE PARENTAL SPIRIT
> SIMPLY WILL NOT HEAR IT.

BOBBY'S DAD.
>WHENEVER YOU GET A LITTLE DOWN
>AND THINK THAT YOUR HARD LUCK LIFE WILL NEVER TURN AROUND
>JUST REMEMBER THE FLOWERS THAT FIRST BLOOM LATE IN SPRING
>LET THE THOUGHT OF THEIR BEAUTY NUMB THE STING

FAITH'S MOM.
>WHENEVER YOU FEEL YOUR DAY WON'T COME
>AND MAYBE SUCCESS AND FAME ARE NOT FOR EVERYONE
>REMEMBER THE PEOPLE THAT GOT STARTED LATE IN SPRING
>THEN A LATEBLOOMER'S SAMBA, YOU'LL START TO SING
>
>DR. PHIL
>WAS OVER THE HILL
>THOUGH HE GOT DISMISSED BY SOME
>HE WAS BALD, HE WASN'T DUMB
>AND WHEN OPRAH CALLED HIM CHUM
>NO ONE NOTICED HIS HAIR

FAITH'S MOM.
>DR. RUTH WAS FAR FROM A YOUTH
>WHEN SHE CASHED HER FIRST BIG CHECKS
>PUT THE ACCENT ON GOOD SEX
>AND SHE SAID IT'S NOT COMPLEX
>YOU'LL LOVE IT I SWEAR

ALL.
>IT JUST GOES TO SHOW
>YOU NEVER REALLY KNOW
>WHEN IT'S YOUR TIME
>YOUR TIME TO SHINE
>
>*(Dance break – **FAITH** and **BOBBY** join in.)*

BOBBY'S DAD.
>WHENEVER YOU TRY TO START AGAIN
>AND THINK THAT YOU MIGHT FALL SHORT.
>JUST STOP YOURSELF AND THEN
>PICTURE THE BLOSSOMS THAT TAKE THEIR OWN SWEET TIME
>LET A LATEBLOOMER'S SAMBA FILL YOUR MIND

JULIA CHILD WAS HARDLY A CHILD
WHEN SHE WROTE HER FIRST BIG BOOK
AND SHE SOLD A MILLION – LOOK
WHAT THE LADY DID BY COOKING
WITH BUTTER AND WINE

BOBBY'S DAD & FAITH'S MOM.
> IT JUST GOES TO SHOW
> YOU NEVER REALLY KNOW
> WHEN IT'S YOUR TIME
> YOUR TIME TO SHINE

FAITH.
> SO THE NEXT TIME SOMEBODY SAYS
> I'M A LITTLE PAST MY PRIME

BOBBY.
> THINK OF ALL THE FOLKS
> WHO TOOK THEIR OWN SWEET TIME

BOBBY'S DAD.
> LIKE PAUL GAUGIN

FAITH'S MOM.
> AND CEZANNE

BOBBY.
> EUBIE BLAKE BUT NOT CHOPIN

BOBBY'S DAD.
> FRANK LLOYD WRIGHT

FAITH'S MOM.
> AND FRANK GEHRY

FAITH.
> STOOGES CURLY, MOE AND LARRY

BOBBY'S DAD.
> COLONEL SANDERS

BOBBY.
> GRANDMA MOSES

SHIRLEY.
> AND THAT MOM OF GYPSY ROSE'S

ALL.
>WHO SHOWED THE WORLD
>IT'S NEVER TOO LATE
>FOR THE LATEBLOOMER'S SAMBA
>TO TAKE YOU THERE!

6. I'M MAD AS HELL

(**JAMES** *is at sofa,* **BOBBY** *and* **GLENN** *are at the counter,* **FAITH** *is at window seat.*)

(**JAMES** *is seated at a laptop computer. He is having trouble. The computer noises become hip-hop rhythms.* **JAMES** *dances…badly.*)

JAMES.
> I'M A HARVARD MAN
> I GOT A COLLEGE DEGREE
> BUT I CAN'T KEEP UP
> WITH ALL THIS NEW TECHNOLOGY
> I'M A HARVARD MAN
> AN EDUCATED GUY
> BUT COMPUTERS CHANGE
> IN THE BLINK OF AN EYE
> AND THEY'RE PASSIN' ME BY
> AND I JUST WANNA CRY
> I'M A HARVARD MAN…I'M A HAR…I'M A HAR…

GLENN & BOBBY. Stop it! Stop it right now! Cease! Desist!

(**JAMES** *shuts the computer off.*)

GLENN. What the heck are you doing?

JAMES. Yo my bad peeps! I ain't doin' – I'm bein'! I'm hip. I'm hip – hop – happenin'. I'm all that plus a bag of potato chips.

BOBBY. Who are you supposed to be? Droop Doggy Dogg?

JAMES. Whoa! Gimme my props! Is the implification that I be too old to rap?

GLENN. No, the implifi…the impli…the…

JAMES. Spill it, my brother.

BOBBY. What he's trying to say is you're too rhythmless to rap.

GLENN. And you're not nearly angry enough. Maybe you're running low on caffeine. We'll get you a refill.

(**BOBBY** *and* **GLENN** *exit.*)

JAMES. *(to them as they leave)* I can do anger, alright…all day and all night. Big time! Anger is the roommate at my crib!

(**JAMES** *turns the computer back on; hip-hop rhythm resumes.*)

I TRY TO STAY ON TOP OF THE LEARNING CURVE
BUT I LOSE MY NERVE AND I START TO SWERVE
I BOUGHT A NEW LAPTOP – IT'S S'POSED TO BE A SNAP
BUT I WANNA SMASH IT AND TURN IT INTO SCRAP

(**JAMES** *takes out a cell phone and pushes a button. To the audience.*)

Speed dial.

(A telephone ring is heard.)

GLENN (SOFTWARE TECHNICIAN). *(speaking with a heavy Indian accent [prerecorded])* Hello. Microsoft tech support. How may I service you?

JAMES.
I TELL HIM MY PROBLEM
BUT THERE'S NO COMMUNICATION
AND THREE HOURS LATER
I'M FILLED WITH FRUSTRATION

I'M MAD, I'M ANGRY, I'M STEAMED, I'M IRATE
I WANNA THROW SOME PLATES AT BILL GATES
I'M FURIOUS AT WINDOWS, I LOATHE INTEL
I JUST DON'T GET IT AND I'M MAD AS HELL
MY PATIENCE IS GONE – I CAN'T TAKE ANY MORE
I GOTTA MAKE ANOTHER TRIP TO THE COMPUTER STORE

Maybe somebody there speaks English.

(**JAMES** *picks up the laptop and puts a boombox on his shoulder. The hip-hop beat continues as he dances across the stage to the computer store. He reads a sign…*)

"The Einstein Corner." Okay! Sounds like my kinda place.

(**BOBBY** *and* **JAMES** *are behind the counter, dressed like computer nerds.*)

BOBBY. Can we help you, sir?

JAMES. I'm getting the Rush Limbaugh show broadcast through my modem and I can't get online.

GLENN. Let's take a look at it.

(He opens it and turns it on.)

This is an old, old operating system. Ancient even.

BOBBY. I've never even seen this model.

JAMES. I just bought it two weeks ago!

GLENN. Yeah, it's obsolete.

BOBBY. We only handle the new stuff here.

GLENN. But we do offer free weekly tutoring sessions for people of a certain age to help them feel a little more current.

JAMES.
    I'M GONNA DRIVE MYSELF CRAZY
    ON THE INFORMATION HIGHWAY
    DON'T WANNA SEEM LAZY
    BUT I'M GONNA DO IT MY WAY
    I'LL HIRE AN ASSISTANT
    TO MAKE ME LOOK COOL

    I'M SURE I CAN FIND ONE
    AT THE LOCAL GRADE SCHOOL
    THEN I'LL BID MY COMPUTER
    A FOND FAREWELL
    'CAUSE I JUST DON'T GET IT
    AND I'M MAD AS HELL

BOBBY & GLENN.
    HE JUST DOESN'T GET IT
    AND HE'S MAD AS HELL
    HE JUST DOESN'T GET IT
    AND HE'S MAD AS HELL
    HE JUST DOESN'T GET IT
    AND HE'S MAD AS HELL

(They all continue with rap chant as they exit.)

JAMES. Word – Perfect!

7. CRUSH

FAITH. *(entering with a notebook and textbook)*
I GOTTA GET A JOB
I GOTTA PAY MY RENT
I GOTTA LEARN NEW SKILLS
I GOTTA REINVENT
SO THE NEXT FEW MONTHS ARE GONNA BE SPENT
AT BEVERLY HILLS HIGH SCHOOL!

(Fantasy "time warp" music. The **MEN** *set up the classroom as they spookily intone "Hiiiiiigh school!")*

THE SIGHTS, THE SOUNDS, THE SMELLS
THE BELLS THAT CHIME
IT'S LIKE A SENTIMENTAL JOURNEY BACK IN TIME
THE LOCKERS IN THE HALLS
THE POSTERS ON THE WALLS
THE FILTHY DRINKING FOUNTAINS
THE GRAFFITIED BATHROOM STALLS

ALL.
NOW WE SIT IN THIS FAMILIAR MENTAL WARD
WAITING FOR THE TEACHER TO TORTURE US
HE WALKS IN THE ROOM, WRITES HIS NAME ON THE BOARD

FAITH.
AND OH, MY GOD
HE'S ABSOLUTELY GORGEOUS!

TEACHER (OFFSTAGE VOICE). Buenos tardes, estudiantes. Welcome to Spanish 101. Me llamo Señor Morales.

MEN.
AH HAH

FAITH.
HOW CAN THE TEACHER BE SO COOL?
I'M LIKE A LOVESICK KID IN SCHOOL
MY HEART POUNDS

MEN.
OOH!

FAITH.
I'M WEAK-KNEED

MEN.
>AH!

FAITH.
>MY THOUGHTS RACE

MEN.
>OH!

FAITH.
>AT FULL SPEED

MEN.
>OW!

FAITH.
>I CAN'T BREATHE
>AND I FEEL AN INCREDIBLE RUSH

MEN.
>OOH OOH

FAITH.
>MAYBE I'M …

ALL.
>…CRAZY
>BUT YOU'RE NEVER TOO OLD FOR A CRUSH

MEN.
>AH HAH

FAITH.
>AND WHEN HE LOOKS MY WAY IN CLASS
>THE WHOLE WORLD SPINS – I'M FALLIN' FAST
>OUR HANDS TOUCH

MEN.
>OOH!

FAITH.
>OUR EYES MEET

MEN.
>AH!

FAITH.
>I'M SQUIRMIN'

MEN.
>OH!

FAITH.
> IN MY SEAT

MEN.
> OW!

ALL.
> HE SMILES SWEET

FAITH.
> AND MY FACE IS BEGINNING TO BLUSH

MEN.
> OOH OOH OOH

FAITH.
> MAYBE I'M

ALL.
> …CRAZY
> BUT YOU'RE NEVER TOO OLD FOR A CRUSH

MEN.
> OOH OOH OOH

FAITH.
> WOULD I BE BETTER OFF TO…

MEN.
> DROP OUT
> A – HAH

FAITH.
> FEELIN' THESE FEELINGS I CAN'T…

MEN.
> STOMP OUT
> MAYBE HE'LL BREAK YOUR FOOLISH HEART

FAITH.
> BUT THAT MIGHT EVEN BE THE BEST

MEN.
> THE VERY BEST

FAITH.
> YES, THE VERY BEST

ALL.
> BETTER THAN ALL OF THE REST PART
> AH, AH AH AH AH

FAITH.
> OOH OOH OOH OOH OOH
> OOH OOH OOH OOH
> AND WHEN HE SMILES, I UNDERSTAND
> LIFE NEVER GOES JUST LIKE WE PLANNED
> I'M HUMAN

MEN.
> YEAH!

FAITH.
> SO SUE ME

MEN.
> NAH!

FAITH.
> LET THIS ANGEL

MEN.
> ALL RIGHT!

FAITH.
> RENEW ME

MEN.
> DO ME...BABY

FAITH. *(overlapping)*
> LIKE A BABY, I TURN INTO A PUDDLE OF MUSH
> THESE FEELINGS AMAZE ME
> THAT SOMEONE CAN STILL DAZE ME
> MAYBE I'M CRA-YAY-YAY-YAY-ZY

Crazy – I mean loco – about you, Señor Morales.

> BUT YOU'RE NEVER TOO OLD FOR A...

MEN.
> ...CRU-USH

FAITH.
> OOH OOH OOH OOH OOH, OOH OOH OOH

8. THE ROAD NOT TAKEN

(**SHIRLEY** *enters carrying a box. She sets it down on a table and approaches the* **BARISTA**.)

SHIRLEY. Hey Barry – I brought those things I told you about. Thanks for letting me unload them.

(*The barista nods okay.* **SHIRLEY** *addresses the audience as she sets various objects on the shelves.*)

My neat-freak husband gave me a deadline to go through the "stuff" in the storage closet and finally decide what to keep, or he's threatened to rent a bulldozer and take it all away. I don't think of myself as sloppy, exactly – just organizationally challenged.

(*taking out a book*)

The Feminine Mystique. That rocked our world.

(*opening it*)

Oh, my god…it's signed by Betty Friedan! "To Shirley…" How could I have forgotten? I'm not gettin' rid of that.

(*She puts it back in the box.*)

A playbill from *Hair.* I played the part of…what was her name?

(*looking inside*)

Sheila! In the Berkeley production. Of course, I opted to do the nude scene. Just to drive my parents crazy.

(*She puts the playbill back in the box and takes out a framed photo.*)

Here's a frightening thought… Our high school class is running the country now. Of course, we thought we could run it back then. We were going to change the world with coffee-house politics and protest songs.

I FOUND AN OLD PICTURE OF ME IN A DRAWER
I WAS ANGRY, BEING LED OFF BY POLICE
DEFIANT IN MY JANE FONDA SHAG

SHIRLEY. *(cont.)*
PROTESTING THE WAR
DISTURBING THE PEACE

AND IN THE SCREAMING CROWD BEHIND MY FIST
I STILL CAN SEE HIS TANNED AND LOVELY FACE
WE WERE LOVERS IN THAT SNAPSHOT OF MY YOUTH
NOW BLURRED BY TIME AND SPACE

THE ROAD NOT TAKEN
SO LONG AGO
WAS I MISTAKEN?
THE VOICE OF REASON IN MY HEAD SAYS NO
BUT THERE'S A WHISPER
INSIDE MY HEART

AND IF YOU LISTEN
YOU MIGHT HEAR IT BREAK
FOR THE ROAD I DIDN'T TAKE

ONE SUMMER, ANOTHER MAN ENTERED MY LIFE
AS DIFFERENT FROM THE FIRST ONE AS COULD BE
WITH PERFECT HAIR AND CUSTOM-TAILORED SUITS
OH, I WAS SO SURE HE WASN'T FOR ME

BUT SOMEHOW WHEN I LOOKED BEHIND HIS SMILE
I SAW A GENTLE STRENGTH THAT TURNED THE TIDE
THROUGH THE FIGHTS AND COMPROMISES THAT WE'VE
    MADE
HE'S NEVER LEFT MY SIDE

THE ROAD I'VE TAKEN
THE CHOICE I MADE
OLD FIRES AWAKEN
I'M CERTAIN I WOULD NEVER MAKE THE TRADE

BUT THERE'S THAT WHISPER
THAT COMES AND GOES
THAT SMALL REMINDER
OF THE LIFE YOU'D MAKE
ON THE ROAD YOU DIDN'T TAKE

NO ONE ELSE HAS EVER REALLY KNOWN
THAT UNTAMED GIRL

SHIRLEY. *(cont.)*
>EXCEPT THAT BOY, SO BOLD AND ROUGH
>HE WAS THE LOVE OF MY LIFE
>BUT SOMETIMES LOVE IS NOT ENOUGH
>
>THE ROAD NOT TAKEN
>THE THINGS YOU LEAVE BEHIND
>THE DREAMS FORSAKEN
>AND THOUGH YOUR HEART WON'T BREAK
>STILL YOU FEEL THE ACHE
>FOR THE ROAD YOU DIDN'T TAKE

9. YOGAROBICS

(**FAITH** *is sitting in a yoga position, and* **GLENN**, **BOBBY** *and* **JAMES** *play the other students.*)

OFFSTAGE VOICE. Welcome to "Yogarobics" – the fusion class for busy people who seek enlightenment while achieving physical fitness. Breathe deeply and see yourself warming up.

FAITH.
>I AM SITTING
>ON A MOUNTAIN
>THE SKY IS CLEAR
>AND I AM GETTING SUNBURNED

OFFSTAGE VOICE. Now imagine yourself in light aerobic motion.

FAITH.
>I AM WALKING
>IN A FOREST
>A GENTLE BREEZE
>BLOWS DIRT BENEATH MY EYELID

OFFSTAGE VOICE. Visualize yourself engaging in more vigorous exercise.

FAITH.
>I AM SWIMMING
>IN THE OCEAN
>THE DOLPHINS PLAY
>OR ARE THOSE SHARKS APPROACHING?
>
>WOULDN'T IT BE EASIER
>IF WE GOT UP
>AND ACTUALLY EXERCISED?
>OR IS THAT JUST DUMB?
>
>AND AS IF I'M NOT
>ALREADY HOT ENOUGH
>THE ROOM IS LIKE A MICROWAVE
>AND MY BUTT IS NUMMMMMMMB

10. DOG PASSAGES

GLENN. *(to his offstage wife)* Honey, I'm going to clean out the garage to make room for the new Sequoia!
A big man needs a big car! She knows why I'm really out here –

(to his dog)

It's to see you. I know you can't help it, but we've got new carpeting and this is your new bedroom. I fought for you big guy, but if it's between sleeping in the garage or wearing diapers, you'd much rather sleep here, right? And I know how to fix this place up. Trust me, you're gonna love it!

THE FIRST DOG I HAD, I INHERITED
A SWEET LITTLE PUG I NAMED SAM
HE WAS THERE WHEN I GOT MY FIRST REAL JOB
MY APARTMENT, AND MY FIRST GIRLFRIEND PAM

I REMEMBER HOW JEALOUS OL' SAM WOULD GET
WHEN PAM AND I CUDDLED AT NIGHT
HE'D CLIMB UP BETWEEN US, THEN START TO GROWL
NOT LETTING ME OUT OF HIS SIGHT
BUT HE LIKED A GIRL DOG WHO LIVED ON THE FIRST FLOOR
HE'D HOWL LIKE A WOLF WHEN WE'D PASS BY HER DOOR
AND SOMETIMES HE'D BREAK FREE JUST LOOKIN' TO SCORE
HIGH ON THE SCENT OF NEW WORLDS TO EXPLORE

AND I LOVED HIM - MORE THAN HE'LL EVER KNOW
AND WHEN HE LEFT, IT WAS HARD LETTING GO
'CAUSE IT WASN'T JUST SAM WHO HAD RUN AWAY
BUT A BOY IN HIS TWENTIES OR SO

DOG PASSAGES, DOG PASSAGES
THAT'S HOW I MARK MY PLACE IN TIME
I DON'T DO IT WITH YEARS OR THE LOVES THAT I'VE LOST
I DO IT WITH ALL THAT'S CANINE – DOG PASSAGES

(takes out a toy)

GLENN. *(cont.)*
NOW MY SECOND DOG, I BOUGHT FOR MY WIFE
AN APRICOT POODLE – FIFI
SHE HAD HER HEART SET ON THIS MINIATURE PET
BUT FROM THE FIRST MOMENT, FIFI LIKED ME

SHE'D TURN UP HER NOSE WHEN MY WIFE COOKED HER MEALS
BUT THE FOOD FROM MY PLATE TASTED GOOD
SHE HAD HER OWN TOYS THAT SHE NEVER WOULD SHARE
BUT SHE'D SHARE THEM WITH ME IF SHE COULD
AND ON WARM SUMMER EVENINGS WE'D PLAY IN THE YARD
SHE WAS A SMALL DOG, BUT SHE HAD A BIG HEART

AND I LOVED HER - MORE THAN SHE'LL EVER KNOW
WHEN SHE DIED IN MY ARMS, WHAT A TERRIBLE BLOW
'CAUSE IT WASN'T JUST FIFI WHO'D PASSED AWAY
BUT A MAN IN HIS THIRTIES OR FORTIES OR SO

DOG PASSAGES, DOG PASSAGES
THAT'S HOW I MARK MY PLACE IN TIME
I DON'T MEASURE MY LIFE BY THE THINGS THAT I OWN
MY MEMORIES MOSTLY DEFINE – DOG PASSAGES

(He takes out an old Frisbee.)

THE DOG I HAVE NOW IS A MUTT I SAVED
WHO'S GROWN A BIT LONG IN THE TOOTH
I SPEND HALF MY TIME TAKIN' CARE OF HIM
LET'S FACE IT, HE'S NOT IN HIS YOUTH

BUT BUTCH DOESN'T FEEL MUCH LIKE GOIN' OUT
HE LURCHES FROM PILLAR TO POST
AND I HAVE TO CHOP ALL HIS DOGGIE FOOD
'CAUSE HIS TEETH IN THE FRONT ARE JUST TOAST

AND HE DROOLS ON MY PILLOW, HE PEES ON THE FLOOR
BUT WHEN I COME HOME, HE'S RIGHT THERE BY THE DOOR

AND I LOVE HIM - MORE THAN HE'LL EVER KNOW
WHAT WILL I DO WHEN IT'S HIS TURN TO GO?
'CAUSE IT'S NOT JUST OLD BUTCH WHO WILL PASS AWAY
BUT A MAN NEARIN' 50 – WELL, 50 OR SO

GLENN. (cont.)
DOG PASSAGES, DOG PASSAGES
A JOURNEY WITH SOME FRIENDS OF MINE
I COULD DRAW YOU A CHART OR A MAP OF MY HEART
TRACING THE REASON AND RHYME
PAW BY PAW, TAIL BY TAIL, NOSE BY NOSE – WELL, HERE GOES!

SNIFFIN' OUT LIFE'S INFINITE MESSAGES
DOG BY DOG BY DOG – DOG PASSAGES
THAT'S HOW I MARK MY PLACE IN TIME

(He tosses the Frisbee offstage.)

Here, Butch! Fetch!

(pause)

That's okay, boy – I can still get it for you.

*(**GLENN** exits.)*

11. AGE IS JUST A NUMBER

*(**BOBBY**, **JAMES**, **SHIRLEY** and **FAITH** are at the coffee bar.)*

BOBBY. Maybe my dad is right. I can't keep dancing forever. I can still do what I did onstage when I was 24, I just can't do it eight times a week anymore.

JAMES. Well then, what are you going to do?

BOBBY. I've got my feelers out to see if I can segue into being a choreographer. Hell, I've thought I could do it better than most of them for years anyway – maybe 50 really is too old for the chorus.

FAITH. I don't think of myself as 50. I'm 27 with 23 years of experience.

*(**GLENN** enters.)*

JAMES. Dream on sister.

GLENN. Well Faith, I think it's a beautiful thought.

SHIRLEY. And anyway, everyone knows that 50 is the new 40. And with all the new surgical procedures, cosmetics, nutrition and social attitudes – pretty soon 60 will be the new 30.

JAMES. Hey, the way things are going, eventually 70 will be the new 10! I could still have a shot at being a child prodigy!

BOBBY. Oh, who are we kidding? 50 is the new 50!

*(to **SHIRLEY**)*

ARE MY TEETH GETTING A LITTLE YELLOW?
IS MY CHINLINE TURNING TO JELL-O?
AM I LOOKING A LITTLE TOO DISTINGUISHED?
IS MY BOYISH LOOK ALL BUT EXTINGUISHED?

SHIRLEY.
WHAT HAVE YOU GOT TO COMPLAIN ABOUT?
SO YOU'LL NEVER PASS FOR FORTY AGAIN
BUT KID, YOU LOOK TERRIFIC
WE ALL HAVE BIRTHDAYS EVERY TWELVE MONTHS
BUT THAT'S JUST SO HALLMARK CAN SELL SOME CARDS

SHIRLEY. *(cont.)*
IT ONLY MATTERS HOW YOU FEEL INSIDE
AND NOT HOW OLD YOU ARE!

I KNEW A MAN WHO WAS SIXTY
WHO WAS AS SHARP A BOY OF TWENTY
I KNEW A BOY OF TWENTY – THAT'S RIGHT
WHOSE MIND WAS ALL COBWEBBED AND FUNNY
ISN'T IT STRANGE HOW LITTLE WE CHANGE
ON THE INSIDE AS THE DAYS GO BY
DON'T LET THE MIRROR FOOL YOU NONE
IT'S JUST A LOW-DOWN, DIRTY, ROTTEN LIE
AGE IS JUST A NUMBER

ALL OTHERS.
AGE IS JUST A NUMBER

SHIRLEY.
NO MATTER WHAT THE WORLD HAS SAID
YOU MIGHT THINK IT'S OVER

ALL.
BUT BETTER THINK IT OVER
AND CHANGE YOUR POINT OF VIEW INSTEAD

SHIRLEY.
I DON'T FEEL ANY DIFFERENT THAN I DID
WHEN I WAS A KID OF TWENTY-FIVE
AGE IS JUST A NUMBER

ALL.
AGE IS JUST A NUMBER

SHIRLEY.
AND THE REST IS JUST A BUNCH OF JIVE
I KNOW THE BODY STARTS SHIFTIN'

MEN.
SHIFTIN'

SHIRLEY.
CRAZY LINES MAKE…

ALL.
…DESIGNS ON YOUR FACE

SHIRLEY.
> TIME HAS A WAY OF LIFTIN' YOU UP
> GIVIN' YOU WISDOM AND A HARD-WON GRACE
> DON'T THINK YOUR MIND IS FALLIN' BEHIND
> 'CAUSE YOUR BEHIND IS FALLIN' DOWN LOW
> PICK YOURSELF UP AND STRUT YOUR BAD STUFF
> WE'VE ALL GOT A LONG, LONG WAY TO GO
> AGE IS JUST A NUMBER

COMPANY.
> AGE IS JUST A NUMBER

SHIRLEY.
> NO MATTER WHAT YOU'VE SEEN OR READ
> YOU MIGHT THINK "WHY BOTHER?"

BOBBY.
> I COULD BE THEIR FATHER

ALL.
> BUT LISTEN, DADDY – YOU AIN'T DEAD

SHIRLEY.
> NOW DON'T SPEND ALL YOUR SPARE TIME FEELIN' BLUE
> YOU'RE TURNIN' INTO AN AWFUL MESS
> AGE IS JUST A NUMBER

COMPANY.
> FORGET ABOUT THE NUMBER

SHIRLEY.
> THAT'S THE SECRET OF MY SUCCESS

COMPANY.
> 21, 22, 23

SHIRLEY.
> THE WHOLE WORLD MAKES YOU MAD

COMPANY.
> 31, 32, 33, 34

SHIRLEY.
> YOUR GIRLFRIEND TREATS YOU BAD

COMPANY.
> 41, 42, 43, 44, 45

SHIRLEY.
>SUPERMOM'S NOT SO TOUGH
>51, 52, 53, 54, 55, 56

ALL.
>KID STUFF!

SHIRLEY.
>AGE IS JUST A NUMBER

COMPANY.
>AGE IS JUST A NUMBER

SHIRLEY.
>NO MATTER WHAT THE WORLD HAS SAID
>YOU MIGHT THINK IT'S OVER

ALL.
>BUT BETTER THINK IT OVER
>AND CHANGE YOUR POINT OF VIEW INSTEAD

SHIRLEY.
>I DON'T FEEL ANY DIFFERENT THAN I DID
>WHEN I WAS A KID OF TWENTY-FIVE
>AGE IS JUST A NUMBER

COMPANY.
>AGE IS JUST A NUMBER

SHIRLEY.
>AND THE FACT THAT I'VE SURVIVED
>MAKES ME GLAD

COMPANY.
>NO MATTER WHAT PEOPLE HAVE SAID
>THE LADY'S STILL KNOCKIN' 'EM DEAD

SHIRLEY.
>TO BE ALIVE

COMPANY.
>PRETTY SENSATIONAL
>DAMN INSPIRATIONAL

SHIRLEY.
>'CAUSE I STILL CAN

COMPANY.
>GIVE THE LADY A HAND

SHIRLEY.
>AGE IS JUST A NUMBER

ALL.
>OH YEAH!

12. LUNCH HOUR LIFT

*(**SHIRLEY** and **FAITH** enter a coffee bar.)*

FAITH. *(to the **BARISTA**)* I would like uno cafe immenso, por favor. With dos shots – no, tres – wait, make that quatro shots of espresso. A triple pump of mocha flavor and topped with chocolate whipped cream.

SHIRLEY. And I'll just have a…

FAITH. *(interrupting)* With a drizzle of chocolate syrup over it.

SHIRLEY. Give me a…

FAITH. *(interrupting)* And some chocolate sprinkles.

SHIRLEY. Let me have a…

FAITH. *(interrupting)* I'll take a double fudge brownie, too. No fork. Gracias.

*(**SHIRLEY** stares at **FAITH**.)*

FAITH. Go ahead.

SHIRLEY. Are you sure?

*(to the **BARISTA**)*

Cuppa Joe. Black.

FAITH. What about a pastry?

SHIRLEY. No – everything slows down with age, except the time it takes for bakery goods to reach your hips.

FAITH. Yeah, time may be a great healer, but it's a lousy beautician.

SHIRLEY.
I FEEL SAGGY

FAITH. *(to the mirror)*
I FEEL BAGGY

SHIRLEY.
I FEEL HAGGY AND DRAGGY AND BLAH

FAITH. *(moving the mirror to her breasts)*
AND I WONDER
IF I OUGHT TO GET A WONDER BRA

Let's face it – I need a suspension bridge.

SHIRLEY. I don't mean to trivialize your problems, but last week I found an enormous lump halfway down the back of my thigh.

FAITH. Oh, my god! Did you go to the doctor?

SHIRLEY. Yes.

FAITH. What is it?

SHIRLEY. My ass. The good news is, the doctor says he can fix it. And the even better news is, he can do it on my lunch hour.

FAITH. On your lunch hour?! He's got to be putting you on. Anyway, I thought you said age is just a number.

SHIRLEY. It is…and the number is right here in this brochure, under the fee schedules.

    HE'LL STICK A NEEDLE IN MY BUTT AND SUCK THE FAT OUT
    THEN PUT IT IN MY LIPS AND MAKE 'EM PLUMP
    AND HE GUARANTEES IN SIXTY MINUTES FLAT OUT
    I'LL HAVE A SEXY SMILE AND GORGEOUS RUMP

    THE DOCTOR'S COOL AND BREEZY
    HE SAYS IT'S VERY EASY
    NO NEED FOR FEELIN' QUEASY OR CONCERNED

FAITH.
    AND IF YOU DON'T ADORE IT
    THEY PROMISE TO RESTORE IT

SHIRLEY.
    THAT'S RIGHT – HE SAYS THE GOODS CAN BE RETURNED

FAITH.
    DID YOU SEE THE PRICE OF LIPO?
    THAT'S GOTTA BE A TYPO

SHIRLEY.
    IT'S NOT EXACTLY IN THE REALM OF THRIFT
    BUT I'LL SAY IT'S SUCH A DEAL
    WHEN I WALK OUT WITH BUNS OF STEEL
    INSTEAD OF DOING LUNCH
    I'LL DO A LUNCH HOUR LIFT

FAITH. *(taking the brochure from* **SHIRLEY***)* Let me see that. Oh, wow – look at this.
THEY'LL CARVE A COUPLE POUNDS OF BACON OFF MY HOOTERS
AND MAKE 'EM CUTE AND PERKY, FIRM AND ROUND
THE WAY THEY'RE ACTIN' NOW, THEY'RE LIKE COMMUTERS
RIDIN' THE EXPRESS TRAIN TO THE GROUND

SHIRLEY.
THE PROCEDURE'S FUNDAMENTAL
IT'S SAFE AND QUICK AND GENTLE
THE PAIN IS INCIDENTAL, AND IT'S BRIEF

FAITH.
WHAT STARTED AS A D-CUP
FITS NICELY IN A TEACUP
THE ONLY THING THAT'S BIG IS THE RELIEF

OKAY, SO IT'S EXPENSIVE
I'M KIND OF APPREHENSIVE

SHIRLEY.
BUT HONEY, WHEN YOUR BOOBS BEGIN TO DRIFT
IF YOU DON'T WANNA HATE 'EM
YOU GOTTA ELEVATE 'EM

FAITH.
INSTEAD OF DOIN' LUNCH
I'LL DO A LUNCH HOUR LIFT

*(****BOBBY**** enters, dressed as a doctor.* ***JAMES*** *and* ***GLENN*** *are orderlies. They all carry hospital dressing screens.)*

BOBBY. This will only take a few minutes.

*(****JAMES****,* ***GLENN*** *and* ***BOBBY*** *encircle* ***FAITH*** *and* ***SHIRLEY*** *with the screens.)*

You're going to feel…

(flashing an evil grin at the audience)

…just a little discomfort.

(Spooky music and screaming. The "patients" are revealed: ***SHIRLEY****'s butt and* ***FAITH****'s chest are swathed in huge bandages.)*

SHIRLEY.
>ALTHOUGH WE MIGHT LOOK YOUNGER…

FAITH.
>YES, AND THINNER!

SHIRLEY.
>THEY LIE ABOUT HOW MUCH IT'S GONNA HURT

FAITH.
>IF THAT WAS LUNCH, I CAN'T IMAGINE DINNER

SHIRLEY.
>I'M GLAD I DIDN'T ORDER A DESSERT

FAITH.
>I'D LOVE A PERFECT BODY
>BUT THIS ONE'S NOT SO SHODDY

SHIRLEY.
>OUR LUMPS AND BUMPS MAY WELL EXPAND AND SHIFT

FAITH & SHIRLEY.
>BUT THERE WON'T BE ANY SUTURES
>IN EITHER OF OUR FUTURES
>WE'LL LET A CUP OF COFFEE BE OUR LUNCH HOUR LIFT

13. THE CHILD IS FATHER TO THE MAN

(**JAMES** *is at window seat.*)

JAMES. *(Reading a paper. To the audience…)* I see the divorce rate is going down in America. Must be because I stopped getting married. Three wives, three divorces, no kids. But that doesn't mean I don't have family responsibilities. Just not the kind I ever expected.
MY DAD LIVES IN A LOVELY HOME
HE'S DOING VERY WELL
AND WHEN HE WANTS SOME FOOD OR DRINK
HE SIMPLY RINGS A BELL

He loves that!
HE COMPLAINS ABOUT THE MEALS THEY BRING
SAYS HE DOESN'T WANT TO STAY
SO EVERY OTHER WEEKEND I TAKE HIM OUT
THOUGH I LIVE SO FAR AWAY

(**GLENN** *enters, dressed as* **DAD**.)

DAD.
GOD, THIS PLACE IS AN AWFUL DUMP
THE NURSES HIDE MY CANE
WHEN I CALL FOR THEM, THEY NEVER COME

What do they know about pain?
ONCE OR TWICE A MONTH, MY KID DROPS IN
THOUGH HE'S LIVING REAL NEARBY
HE ASKS THE SAME DAMN QUESTIONS
SO HALF THE TIME I LIE

JAMES & DAD.
AS A FAMILY, IT'S JUST THE TWO OF US
IN THE BUFFET LINE AT 4 P.M.

DAD.
I TELL MY KID ALL THE LATEST JOKES

JAMES.
AND I LAUGH AT THEM…AGAIN
HE DOESN'T ASK ABOUT MY LIFE

DAD.
HE LEAVES TOO BIG A TIP

JAMES.
>WE'RE AWKWARDLY POLITE AND COOL

JAMES & DAD.
>LIKE STRANGERS ON A SHIP

JAMES.
>SO ISN'T IT IRONIC THAT HE NEEDS ME
>AS A FRIEND

DAD. No!
>AS A SON

JAMES.
>AFTER A LIFE OF STUBBORN INDEPENDENCE

DAD.
>I NEVER NEEDED ANYONE

JAMES.
>THE CHILD IS FATHER TO THE MAN
>FUNNY HOW THE ROLES REVERSE
>WHETHER YOU LIKE IT OR NOT, THAT'S THE WAY IT IS
>YOU'RE THEIR CHAUFFEUR, COMPANION AND NURSE
>
>THE CHILD IS FATHER TO THE MAN
>SOMETIMES IT'S ALL SO CLEAR
>THE MOMENTS WHEN WE DO CONNECT
>THAT'S WHY I'M STILL HERE

DAD. *(overlapping)*
>I'M NOT A CHILD
>I'M STILL YOUR DAD.
>WE DON'T CONNECT, WE NEVER DID
>YOU'RE STILL MY KID

JAMES.
>AND YOU'RE NEVER SURE JUST WHAT TO DO
>WHEN THE CHILD BECOMES THE FATHER TO THE MAN
>
>HEY! I BROUGHT A SNAPSHOT OF MOM AND HIM
>ON THE BOARDWALK IN '41

DAD.
>BUT WHEN HE LEFT, I PUT IT AWAY
>WHAT'S IN THE PAST IS DONE

JAMES.
>YOU ALWAYS THINK YOU KNOW IT ALL

DAD.
>PICKIN' FIGHTS WITH YOUR OLD MAN?
>MAYBE I WON'T PUT IN MY HEARING AID

JAMES.
>YEAH, YOU ANNOY ME THE BEST YOU CAN
>
>SO ISN'T IT IRONIC THAT HE NEEDS ME
>SO I STICK AROUND, YOU SEE

DAD. (*overlapping*)
>WHO NEEDS YOU?
>I WISH YOU'D GO AWAY

JAMES.
>HE'S SO STUBBORN AND INDEPENDENT

DAD. Yeah?
>MAYBE SOMEDAY YOU'LL BE MORE LIKE ME

JAMES.
>I'M A LOT LIKE YOU

DAD.
>HE'S A LOT LIKE ME

JAMES.
>THE CHILD IS FATHER TO THE MAN
>AND ITS NOT JUST SOME CLICHÉ

DAD. (*overlapping*)
>NOT JUST SOMETHING THEY SAY

JAMES.
>IT'S THE STONE COLD TRUTH, A FACT OF LIFE

JAMES & DAD.
>I LIVE WITH EVERY DAY

DAD.
>THE CHILD IS FATHER TO THE MAN
>SOMETIMES IT'S AN AWFUL CURSE

JAMES.
>HE'S GOT HIS MOODS, YOU JUST CAN'T WIN

DAD.
>THINGS GO FROM BAD TO WORSE

JAMES & DAD.
>IN THIS WHOLE DAMN UNIVERSE
>THE TWO OF US GROWING OLD TOGETHER

JAMES.
> GOD MUST BE…

DAD.
> PERVERSE

JAMES.
> OR MAYBE IT'S ALL PLANNED
> AND WE'RE NOT MEANT TO UNDERSTAND

JAMES & DAD.
> SO YOU DO THE VERY BEST YOU CAN

JAMES.
> AND THE CHILD BECOMES THE FATHER TO…

DAD.
> THE CHILD BECOMES THE FATHER TO…

JAMES & DAD.
> THE MAN

14. WHEN 50 WORE A TUX

(**BOBBY** *alone on stage.*)

BOBBY. I always measured time according to the clothes I wore. Another decade? Another reason to go shopping. From the time I was ten, I didn't wear anything that wasn't ironed or dry-cleaned. I learned early on that even if you didn't have anything to your name except a dream, if you dressed the part you were somebody…
AS A FASHION-CONSCIOUS CHILD
I COULDN'T WAIT TILL I WAS GROWN
I'D HAVE A CLOSET FULL OF CLOTHES
OH, WHAT FINERY I'D OWN
IN MY FIRST PAIR OF EVENING PANTS
I'D SIP CHAMPAGNE, AND EVEN DANCE
SO ADULT AND DEBONAIR
LIKE A FULL-HAIRED FRED ASTAIRE
NOW SUCH GRACE IS A FADED MEMORY
HOW I LONG FOR A TRACE OF THE WAY IT USED TO BE

WHEN 50 WORE A TUX
A TOP HAT AND SOME STYLE
MEN LOOKED SO DELUXE
AND EACH YEAR JUST MADE 'EM SMILE
THAT'S HOW I PICTURED I WOULD BE
ENROLLED IN HIGH SOCIETY
LOOKIN' LIKE A MILLION BUCKS
WHEN I WAS 50 AND I WORE MY TUX

WHEN 50 WORE A TUX
A WATCH FOB AND SOME SPATS
MEN LOOKED SO DELUXE
EVEN CRIMINALS WORE HATS
THAT'S HOW I PICTURED I WOULD BE
THE MODEL OF PROSPERITY
LOOKIN' LIKE A MILLION BUCKS
WHEN I WAS 50 AND I WORE MY TUX

BOBBY. *(cont.)*
NOW MOST MEN AT MY AGE
LOOK LIKE THEY'RE JUST KIDS IN SCHOOL
TORN-UP JEANS AND TENNIS SHOES
WHEN DID SLOPPY GET SO COOL?

TODAY YOU CAN'T TELL DAD APART
FROM HIS KIDS WITHOUT A CHART
WITH HIS BACKWARDS BASEBALL CAP
TELL ME, WHAT FOOL THOUGHT OF THAT?
TAKE ME BACK, TAKE ME BACK

(dance break)

WHEN 50 WORE A TUX
WHITE GLOVES AND A CANE
MEN LOOKED SO DELUXE
STROLLING DOWN A SHADY LANE
THAT'S HOW I PICTURED I WOULD BE
PROUD TO BE MY AGE, YOU SEE
LOOKIN' LIKE A MILLION BUCKS

AND NOW I'M 50
AND I'M WEARIN' MY TUX
AND I'M WEARIN' MY TUX
AND I'M WEARIN' MY – TUX!

15. TOO OLD FOR THE CHORUS

*(**GLENN**, **JAMES**, **FAITH** and **SHIRLEY** look at pictures and posters around set, **FAITH** stands in front of an old poster.)*

FAITH. God, when I was a teenager I had that poster over my bed – and I used to think he was so sexy. What's with the hair?

SHIRLEY. Listen, honey that's nothing – back in the 70s I collected Salvador Dali. I even had one of his "Melting Clock" wrist watches – hell, I never knew what the time was.

GLENN. Oh we've all had our run-ins with art. I had my "unicorn" and "frog" phase. My wife put a stop to that. One day they just disappeared.

FAITH. James, I bet you were always in the best of taste.

GLENN. Oh – no, no, no. *(like a radio announcer)* You my friend wore Hi-Karate After Shave.

JAMES. I did not, I wore – Canoe… *(laughing at himself)* and this stupid Fu Manchu moustache that I thought made me look macho.

GLENN. I wore a Dashiki.

SHIRLEY. What's a Dashiki?

GLENN. It's kinda like an African Hawaiian shirt.

JAMES. The things we've lived through.

FAITH. Tiny Tim.

SHIRLEY. Macramé.

JAMES. Mimes.

GLENN. Nehru Jackets.

FAITH. Metallic Wallpaper.

JAMES. *(pause…and then **JAMES** looking wistful says)* Three martini lunches.

SHIRLEY. *(crosses over to **JAMES** and puts her hand on his shoulder)*
THERE COMES A MOMENT
WHEN YOU HAVE TO LEAVE TREASURED THINGS BEHIND

FAITH.
> YOU HAVE TO MAKE SOME SPACE
> TO FILL SOME SPACE
> FOR EACH OF US, IT'S TIME

GLENN.
> SO I'LL FINALLY THROW OUT MY TOO TIGHT SWEATERS

BOBBY.
> DONATE MY OLD PAIR OF PLATFORM SHOES

JAMES.
> I'LL FINALLY DITCH MY BOOM BOX. YES….

ALL.
> WHAT HAVE WE GOT TO LOSE?
> LIKE ACTORS ON A NEW STAGE
> TIME TO STEP UP AND CONFESS OUR AGE.

FAITH. *(to* **BOBBY***)* Okay, you go first.

BOBBY. *(to* **FAITH***)* No, you go.

SHIRLEY. *(to* **FAITH** *and* **BOBBY***)* 65.

BOBBY.
> WE'RE TOO OLD FOR THE CHORUS
> SO MUCH BEFORE US, AS WE ARE

ALL.
> YES, WE'RE TOO OLD FOR THE CHORUS
>
> *(adding two bars of music here…)*
>
> BUT NOT TOO OLD TO BE A STAR.

16. MEN-O-PAUSE RAG

(**GLENN**, **JAMES** and **FAITH** *are sitting at a bar, drinking.* **JAMES** *is wearing a backwards baseball cap.*)

JAMES. Did you hear what the Bartender just said to me?

GLENN. No.

FAITH. What?

JAMES. He said "You know, turning your baseball cap around only lowers your IQ, not your age."

GLENN. Well, if the hat fits…

FAITH. I'm trying to replace the things I've thrown out – but with what?

JAMES. Maybe you can get married again?

GLENN. Oh yeah. It always worked for you.

JAMES. Divorce? –Like you've never considered it.

GLENN. Nope. My little surfer girl still makes my heart come all undone.

JAMES. Doesn't she nag you about your weight?

GLENN. She happens to think it's very sexy, the way I've… filled out.

FAITH. Well, I've only had one divorce and I sure feel like I'm having a crisis. Of course, it could just be my menopause.

GLENN. Maybe that's what you're having, James.

JAMES. Don't laugh, smart guy. You could be right.

FAITH. I don't think so. You have the wrong…equipment.

JAMES. Well, women aren't the only ones who go through "The Change!"

GLENN. Yeah, why do you think they call it MEN-o-pause??
  THE HAIR UPON OUR HEADS JUST UP AND DISAPPEARS
  IT GROWS UPON OUR BACKS, IT SHOWS UP IN OUR EARS
  AND OUR BODY FAT HAS FOUND SOME NEW FRONTIERS
  WHEN MEN DO THE MENOPAUSE RAG

JAMES.
  DON'T EVEN THINK ABOUT A GAME OF BASKETBALL
  FORGET THE SPICY FOOD, FORGET THE ALCOHOL

AND AFTER EVERY MEAL, COUNT YOUR CHOLESTEROL
WHEN MEN DO THE MENOPAUSE RAG

GLENN.
GET ME A SPEEDBOAT OR A FERRARI

JAMES.
SEND ME TO KENYA ON A SAFARI

GLENN & JAMES.
WE NEED A FEW MORE NEW ADVENTURES
BEFORE THOSE HEARING AIDS AND DENTURES

GLENN.
A CERTAIN BODY PART IS SLOWER TO REACT

JAMES.
IT NEEDS A LITTLE TIME, IT NEEDS A LOT OF TACT

JAMES & GLENN.
IT'S NOT SO ROUND OR FIRM
OR EVEN FULLY PACKED
WHEN MEN DO THE MENOPAUSE RAG

SUDDEN CHANGES
GRADUAL CHANGES

ALL.
EVERYBODY'S GOT 'EM

FAITH.
WE FALL OFF A CLIFF

JAMES & GLENN.
WE ROLL DOWN THE HILL

ALL.
BUT WE ALL END UP AT THE BOTTOM

FAITH.
DOIN' THE MENOPAUSE

JAMES & GLENN.
DOIN' THE MENOPAUSE

ALL.
DOIN' THE MENOPAUSE RAG!
Somebody turn back the freakin' clock!

17. QUIET FIRE

(Coffee shop. **SHIRLEY** *is sitting at table reading a brochure and* **BOBBY** *is sitting at counter.)*

SHIRLEY. It's been so long since I've bought clothes for Bill – which one of these do you like?

BOBBY. *(looking at catalog)* I'd pick that one, but my other half Richard would go with that one.

SHIRLEY. Are you sure?

BOBBY. We've been together fifteen years. I'm sure.

SHIRLEY. Fifteen years?

BOBBY. And all my friends said it would never last, but even then, I knew better.

SHIRLEY. Well, Bill and I have been together for 28 years. And his parents said it would never last.

BOBBY. What's your secret?

SHIRLEY. To tell you the truth, I don't know. We're practically polar opposites. But we still like each other – and I think he's the smartest guy I've ever met.

BOBBY. Is he funny? 'Cause that's important.

SHIRLEY. Well, he makes me laugh. Most of the time it's inadvertent. Like when he decides to do home repairs.

BOBBY. Oh, yeah. Well, Richard is very good at that. And I can tell you – even if your name is in lights, it's nice to have someone at home who knows how to change a lightbulb.
BEIN' WITH HIM IS SO COMFORTABLE
ME READIN' A BOOK, HIM JUST BEIN' THERE
THE SIMPLE PLEASURES OF AN ORDINARY NIGHT
LOOKIN' AT HIM IN HIS EASY CHAIR

AND WE FINISH EACH OTHER'S SENTENCES
WE LAUGH LIKE OLD FRIENDS WHO KNOW EACH OTHER WELL
OH, HE'S GOT HIS WAYS AND I'VE GOT TO BE RIGHT

BOBBY. *(cont.)*
BUT SEEING HIM THERE, IT'S SO EASY TO TELL
THAT HE'S MY FINEST GIFT AND SUCCESS
AND ANYONE ELSE WOULD BE SO MUCH LESS
WE'RE THE GREATEST LOVE STORY THAT'S NEVER BEEN TOLD
OUR LOVE IS A FLAME THAT'S NEVER GROWN COLD

WE'VE GOT A QUIET FIRE BURNING ENDLESSLY
NEVER GONNA DIE OUT – IT'S STILL AMAZING TO ME
HOW I GET HIGH OFF THE HEAT OF HIS TOUCH
HOW I STILL WANT HIM AS MUCH AS BEFORE, EVEN MORE
'CAUSE THIS HEART OF MINE NEVER WILL TIRE
OF A QUIET FIRE

SHIRLEY.
SOMETIMES LIFE IS IMPOSSIBLE
THE PUSH AND PULL BETWEEN US TWO
THE SIMPLE STRESSES OF AN ORDINARY DAY
STEALIN' THE JOY FROM THE THINGS WE DO

BUT HE'S ALWAYS BEEN THERE WHEN I'VE NEEDED HIM
THROUGH LAUGHTER AND TEARS, WE'VE GOT A HISTORY
THOUGH NOTHING IS SURE IN THIS CHANGING WORLD
AFTER ALL THESE YEARS, HE'S STILL THE ONE FOR ME

WE'VE GOT A QUIET FIRE BURNING ENDLESSLY
NEVER GONNA DIE OUT – IT'S STILL AMAZING TO ME
HOW I GET HIGH OFF THE HEAT OF HIS TOUCH
HOW I STILL WANT HIM AS MUCH AS BEFORE – EVEN MORE
'CAUSE THIS HEART OF MINE NEVER WILL TIRE

SHIRLEY & BOBBY.
OF A QUIET FIRE
NO, THIS HEART OF MINE NEVER WILL TIRE
OF A QUIET FIRE

18. POTENTIAL

(FAITH and JAMES in coffee shop.)

OFFSTAGE VOICE. Attention customers! "Java The Hut" will be closing in 10 minutes. Thank you for your patronage tonight. May the coarse grind be with you.

GLENN. *(entering)* I just bought a car!

JAMES. *(to FAITH)* What's bigger than a Sequoia?

GLENN. I bought a Prius. I'll have so much room that I can convert my big garage into The Sam and Fifi Shelter For Homeless Dogs. I can take them to the new doggie park up the street.

FAITH. I can help you with that, Glenn.

GLENN. Really? You took a course in how to walk dogs?

FAITH. No, I mean the garage. I took a course in carpentry. I figured the only way to get paid for being a homemaker is to actually make a home. So I'm going to spend the summer with Habitat For Humanity. In Mexico. With Senor Morales' team.

(SHIRLEY and BOBBY enter.)

BOBBY. Oh c'mon, you'd be perfect!

SHIRLEY. No, my acting days are behind me.

FAITH. What are you two talking about?

SHIRLEY. Bobby's been asked to choreograph a new musical.

(ad libs all around)

BOBBY. And it's about the life of Gloria Steinem. Wouldn't she be perfect?

SHIRLEY. No, it's time for me to be on the political stage. I'm running for city council.

BOBBY. I can only imagine what your husband has to say about this.

SHIRLEY. No you can't. He not only fully supports it, he's volunteered to be in charge of campaign finance. What about you, James? Ready to settle down?

JAMES. Settle down? Not me! More like…settling up. Excuse me…my pants are vibrating.

(He takes an iPhone out of his pocket.)

Text message coming in on my new iPhone.

(Showing it off. The others ooh and ah.)

Yes! Thank you. You are looking at the new Western Regional Vice President of Marketing for Apple Computers!

*(to **BARISTA**)*

Barry! Champagne for everybody. The good stuff.

BOBBY. Wow! How'd you swing that?

JAMES. I hired a couple of aging 26 year old computer advisors to put together a very hip personal website for me.
WITH THE LESSONS I'VE LEARNED
AND NO ILLUSIONS AT PLAY
AND THE IMPATIENCE OF MY YOUTH
NO LONGER IN MY WAY

ALL (EXCEPT JAMES.)
IT'S A CRAZY WORLD WE LIVE IN

JAMES. *(overlapping)*
IT'S TIME TO FACE IT

ALL (EXCEPT JAMES).
DO WE FIGHT IT OR JUST GIVE IN?

JAMES. *(overlapping)*
LET'S JUST EMBRACE IT

ALL (EXCEPT JAMES).
WE GOT IT. WE GOT IT

JAMES.
I GOT POTENTIAL
AND EVERY MANNER OF CREDENTIAL
MY SELF ASSURANCE
HAS MORE ENDURANCE
THAN A DECADE AGO

BOBBY. *(slowly, into tempo)*
I GOT POTENTIAL
I GOT THE TALENT THAT'S ESSENTIAL

> I GOT AMBITION
> DON'T NEED PERMISSION
> TO BE IN A SHOW

COMPANY. *(in tempo)*
> THOUGH WE'VE LOST THE BLUSH OF YOUTH
> WE HAVE LEARNED TO TELL THE TRUTH
> IS IT REALLY SO UNCOUTH
> TO STILL WANT MORE?
> WE STILL WANT MORE

GLENN.
> I GOT POTENTIAL
> DON'T NEED TO BRAG - IT"S EVIDENTIAL
> AND WHEN I STRUT IN
> NO ONE WILL BUTT IN
> TELLIN' ME NO

WOMEN.
> THE SKY'S THE LIMIT
> MY LIGHT'LL SHINE – NO ONE CAN DIM IT

MEN.
> I'LL COME OUT BLAZIN'
> IT'S JUST AMAZIN'
> WHAT I CAN DO

COMPANY.
> "POTENTIAL… UNTAPPED POTENTIAL"
> WE'RE AT THE JUNCTURE
> WHERE WE CAN PUNCTURE LIES ABOUT TIME
> THEY WON'T SAY WE'RE INCONSEQUENTIAL
> OR PAST OUR PRIME, CAUSE CONFIDENTIALLY
> WE'RE THE BEST WE COULD EVER BE
> FORGET ABOUT WHAT WE HAVE NOT
> THE QUINTESSENTIAL THING THAT WE HAVE GOT
> IS THE TALENT THAT'S ESSENTIAL
> AND EVERY MANNER OF CREDENTIAL
> NO NEED TO BRAG IT'S EVIDENTIAL
> WE'VE GOT POTENTIAL, POTENTIAL
> POTENTIAL!
> *(Curtain calls over **AGE IS JUST A NUMBER**)*

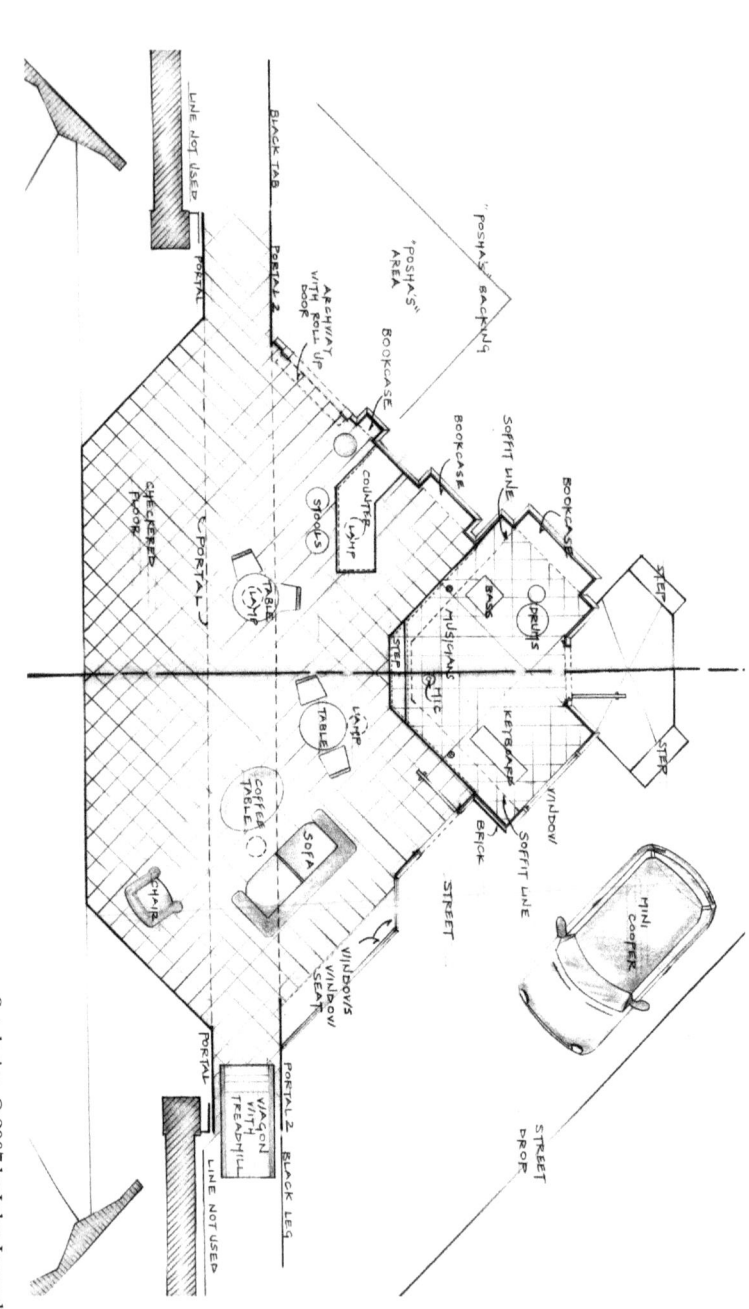

Set design © 2007 by John Iacovelli

OTHER TITLES AVAILABLE FROM SAMUEL FRENCH

THE LAST SESSION

Jim Brochu
Music and Lyrics by Steve Schalchlin
Additional Lyrics by John Bettis and Marie Cain

Musical Comedy / 3m, 2f / Interior

An Off Broadway sensation, *The Last Session* gathers a swinging group in a recording studio to lay down a pop/gospel idol's last album. With one exception, these are old friends (including an ex-wife) and the session is full of warmth, wit, and incredible music. The mix is somewhat altered by a Bible thumping, homophobic gospel singer who is there to replace the one no show of the regular back up singers. All of them, even the sound mixer in the glass booth, are deeply connected to Gideon, yet are unaware that he plans to end his struggle with AIDS after the session. Harmony is restored through friendship and the power of music.

"Exquisite."
– *The New York Times*

"Very affecting…Bright and funny."
– *The New York Post*

"Funny [with] charm and power."
– *New York Daily News*

"The script is full of biting humor [and] the music is incredible…
Guaranteed to move you both musically and emotionally."
– *MTV Online*

"Stirs every emotion in your body."
– *Outlook Magazine*

"Powerful…It touches the heart and tickles the funnybone."
– *Forefront Magazine*

SAMUELFRENCH.COM

OTHER TITLES AVAILABLE FROM SAMUEL FRENCH

HATS! THE MUSICAL

Book by Marcia Milgrom Dodge & Anthony Dodge. Additional Material by Rob Bartlett, Lynne Taylor-Corbett & Sharon Vaughn. Songs by Doug Besterman, Susan Birkenhead, Michele Brourman, Pat Bunch, Gretchen Cryer, Anthony Dodge, Marcia Milgrom Dodge, Beth Falcone, David Friedman, Kathie Lee Gifford, David Goldsmith, Carol Hall, Henry Krieger, Stephen Lawrence, Melissa Manchester, Amanda McBroom, Pam Tillis & Sharon Vaughn

Musical Comedy / 7f

Exploding with fun, *Hats!* is a new musical about a 49.999 year-old woman who reluctantly faces the inevitable BIG 5-0…until she meets several remarkable women who show her about fun, friendship and forgetting about things that simply don't matter anymore.

HATS! features original music by a team of Grammy®, Golden Globe® and Tony® winning songwriters. It is a joyous, provocative, and hilarious evening for everyone who is 50, knows anyone who is 50 or plans to be 50.

"A classy music-and-comedy celebration! It will make a lot of people feel empowered. It does so with integrity, craft, and heart!"
- *Chicago Tribune*

***Hats!* is inspired by the experiences, philosophies, and mission of the Red Hat Society**

SAMUELFRENCH.COM

OTHER TITLES AVAILABLE FROM SAMUEL FRENCH

FUNNY, YOU DON'T LOOK LIKE A GRANDMOTHER

Book and Lyrics by Lois Wise and Sheilah Rae
Music by Robert Waldman

*Musical Comedy Revue / 4 or 5f, 2m / Unit prop set /
1 or 2 pianos + optional band*

Funny, You Don't Look Like a Grandmother is a humorous, heartwarming revue that looks at modern grandmothers in a whole new light. These are the women who have thrown away the granny glasses, shapeless black dresses and Red Cross shoes and replaced them with cute little tennis dresses, skis and a condo in Florida. The show celebrates these changes with skits and songs about everything from what to name the grandmother to her availability as baby sitter, her job, her friends, her activities, her new interest in shopping, but most of all, her relationship to that incredible new baby and its parents. Whether you are a grandparent or a grandchild, every generation of your family will love this show!

"It could be another Nunsense or Forever Plaid — Check it out!"
– Price Berkley, Publisher, *Theatrical Index*

"Funny! This musical revue looks like a winner...laughs for the whole family."
– *The Los Angeles Times*

"Grandmother mixes clever, tuneful songs, a sparklingly witty book, and recognizable characters to serve up a pleasant treat."
– *Miami Herald*

SAMUELFRENCH.COM

www.ingramcontent.com/pod-product-compliance
Lightning Source LLC
Chambersburg PA
CBHW070650300426
44111CB00013B/2352